Cure
QUEST
The Science of **Stem Cell Research**

Stem Cell Research . . . **HEADLINE SCIENCE** . . . Stem Cell Research . . . Headline Science . . .

by Don Nardo

Content Adviser:
Debra Carlson, Ph.D., Department of Biology,
Normandale Community College, Bloomington, Minnesota

Science Adviser:
Terrence E. Young Jr., M.Ed., M.L.S.,
Jefferson Parish (Louisiana) Public School System

Reading Adviser:
Rosemary G. Palmer, Ph.D., Department of Literacy,
College of Education, Boise State University

Compass Point Books • 151 Good Counsel Drive, P. O. Box 669 • Mankato, MN 56002-0669

 This book was manufactured with paper containing at least 10 percent post-consumer waste.

Library of Congress Cataloging-in-Publication Data
Nardo, Don, 1947–
    Cure quest : the science of stem cell research / by Don Nardo.
        p. cm.—(Headline)
    Includes index.
    ISBN 978-0-7565-3371-7 (library binding)
    ISBN 978-0-7565-3374-8 (paperback)
1. Stem cells—Research—Juvenile literature.
2. Embryonic stem cells—Research—Juvenile literature. I. Title. II. Series.
    QH588.S83N37 2009
    616'.02774—dc22   2008005738

Editor: Anthony Wacholtz
Designers: Ellen Schofield and Ashlee Suker
Page Production: Ashlee Suker
Photo Researcher: Eric Gohl

Art Director: LuAnn Ascheman-Adams
Creative Director: Keith Griffin
Editorial Director: Nick Healy
Managing Editor: Catherine Neitge

Photographs ©: Javier Larrea/Art Life Images, cover (bottom), 9; Sven Hoppe/iStockphoto, cover (insert, left), 5; Li Wa/Shutterstock, cover (insert, middle), 16; dra_schwartz/iStockphoto, cover (insert, right), 7; Rawlins–CMSP/Science Faction/Getty Images, 8; Sandy Huffaker/Getty Images, 10, 11; Dr. Cecil H. Fox/Photo Researchers, Inc., 13; 3D4Medical.com/Getty Images, 14; AP Images/*East Valley Tribune*, Thomas Boggan, 15; Stanford University/Getty Images, 19; Library of Congress, 20; Victoria Neis, 21; Louie Psihoyos/Science Faction/Getty Images, 22; Chip Somodevilla/Getty Images, 23; Brandon Laufenberg/iStockphoto, 24; Mark Wilson/Getty Images, 25; Landon Nordeman/Getty Images for Newsweek, 26; Stephen Jaffe/AFP/Getty Images, 27; Seoul National University/Getty Images, 29; Scott Olson/Getty Images, 30; F. Stuart Westmorland/Photo Researchers, Inc., 31; Getty Images, 32; James King-Holmes/Photo Researchers, Inc., 33; Karen Kasmauski/Science Faction/Getty Images, 34; AP Images/Paul Sakuma, 35; Alex Wong/Getty Images, 37; AP Images/Dennis Cook, 38; Shawn Thew/Getty Images, 39; David McNew/Getty Images, 40; AP Images/Andrew Parsons/PA Wire, 41; AP Images/Mike Gullett, 43.

Visit Compass Point Books on the Internet at *www.compasspointbooks.com*
or e-mail your request to *custserv@compasspointbooks.com*

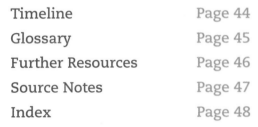

REEVE'S LEGACY: STEM CELL RESEARCH

>> ============> MSNBC
October 11, 2004

The legacy of actor Christopher Reeve won't be for soaring through the air and leaping tall buildings as Superman, but for bringing public attention to spinal cord research while in a wheelchair, medical experts say.

His greatest role was as a champion of sufferers of spinal cord injuries and an advocate of stem cell research.

———

The courage and determination Reeve displayed in trying to overcome his paralysis from a 1995 horse-riding accident far surpassed any of the feats of the comic book hero.

The human body—and the body of every animal—is made up of many tiny individual units called cells. At birth, a human infant has about 20 billion cells. The average number of cells for an adult is about 70 trillion to 100 trillion. Most cells are specialized—they have specific shapes and functions within the body. For example, nerve cells are long and thin, and they carry messages from the brain to various parts of the body. Blood cells, on the other hand, are doughnut-shaped and carry oxygen throughout the body. There are also muscle cells, liver cells, skin cells, brain cells, and many others—more than 200 cell types in all.

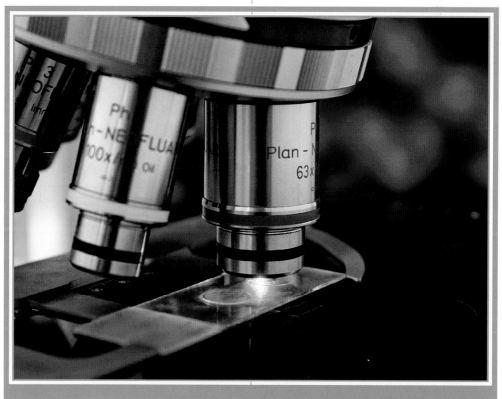

Microscopes are used to magnify images of human cells, which are then transmitted to a computer for analysis.

News changes every minute, and readers need access to the latest information to keep current. Here are a few key search terms to help you locate up-to-the-minute stem cell headlines:

James Thomson

latest stem cells

Parkinson's disease and
  stem cells

regenerative medicine

stem cells debate

stem cells ethics

stem cells legislation

Stem Cells World Congress

Stem cells are different from all other types of cells because they are unspecialized or undifferentiated. For example, stem cells are like people who have not yet decided what they want to be when they grow up. Such people have the potential to learn to do almost any job. Similarly, the body has not yet given stem cells instructions to become particular kinds of cells. Some will become bone cells, while others will become heart, brain, or liver cells.

There are several different kinds of stem cells. The two main categories are embryonic stem cells and adult stem cells.

HOW EMBRYONIC STEM CELLS FORM

Embryonic stem cells are found inside embryos—groups of cells that exist at an early stage in a human's or animal's development. When a male's sperm unites with a female's egg, the egg becomes fertilized. The fertilized

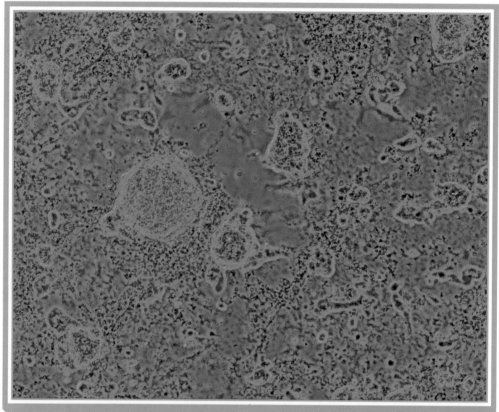

Stem cells are undifferentiated. They have not yet become a specific cell type.

egg begins to grow into a new living organism through cell division. The egg divides into two cells, and each of these cells divides. The embryo then has four cells.

The cells continue to divide, producing more and more cells. Some of these newly created cells are stem cells. When the embryo is between four and eight days old, the stem cells are pluripotent—they are capable of becoming many different cell types. Once a stem cell begins to specialize, or differentiate, it will transform into one type of cell with a specific shape and purpose.

Researchers who want to study and use stem cells do not want the cells to

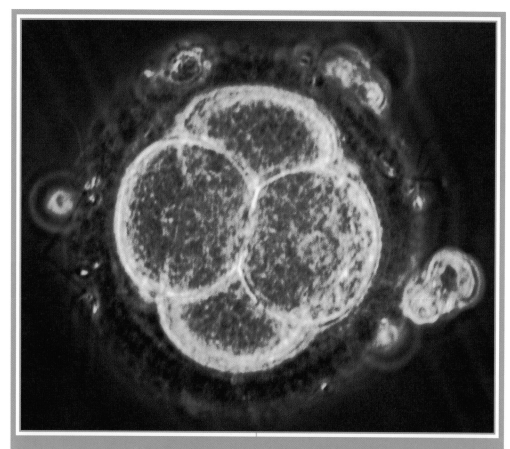

A four-celled embryo is in the early stages of its development. To be used in research, the embryo must continue to divide until there are 40 to 150 cells.

begin differentiation. They must separate the stem cells from the embryo during the pluripotent stage. Using a microscope, the researchers remove the cells from the embryo. Then they place the cells in a round glass container called a petri dish.

ABLE TO REPRODUCE FOREVER?

After transferring the stem cells to the petri dish, the researchers can use them to grow more stem cells because embryonic stem cells easily multiply. All of the stem cells that grow from the first cells taken from an embryo are called a cell line. If scientists take stem cells from a different embryo and multiply them, they create a second cell line. A third embryo will produce a third cell line, and so on. For research purposes, scientists prefer to have several separate cell lines. It is also helpful to have fresh cell lines whenever possible, because the cells in one line can develop defects and other problems over time.

Whichever cell line they are working with, researchers grow the stem cells into a mass of differentiated cells called a tissue. During this process, the goal is to direct the cells to become whatever kind of tissue a medical patient needs. For example, a burn

Stem cells are stored using cryopreservation—a process that keeps the cells unchanged by storing them at extremely low temperatures.

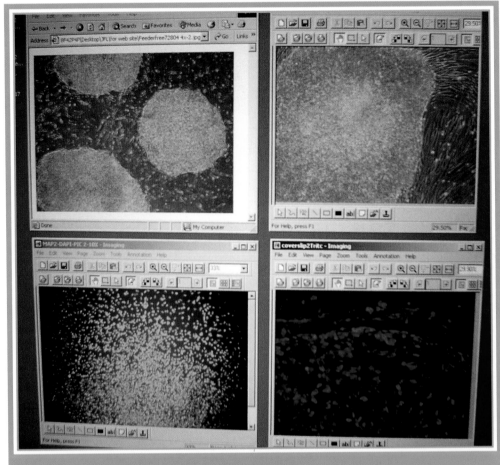

Four stem cell lines are displayed on a computer screen for analysis at the Burnham Institute, a nonprofit, medical research organization in La Jolla, California.

victim's skin tissue has been badly damaged and needs to be replaced. Using chemicals or other means, the researchers hope to direct the stem cells to grow into skin tissue. The new, healthy tissue might then replace the patient's damaged skin.

Scientists are presently seeking ways to grow stem cells into a wide range of human cells, tissues, and organs. In addition to skin tissues, these include blood cells, nerve cells, livers, and kidneys. Growing new nerve cells is especially promising. Many leading scientists and doctors think this will lead to cures for people who are paralyzed or suffer from brain disorders.

Embryologist Ric Ross extracted tissue material from an embryo at the IVF Clinic in California. The clinic accepts donated embryos from around the country.

To make such treatments readily available, one major hurdle still has to be overcome. The patient's body tends to reject these stem cells. This happens because the embryonic stem cells used to grow these new tissues do not usually come from the patient being treated. The person's immune system often sees the new tissues as foreign and rejects them. Doctors are working to find ways to reduce the chance that the body will reject the new cells.

As science writer David E. Newton points out, "Hope for the medical potential of this research is high." Embryonic stem cell research "may provide cures to any number of diseases and disorders that are currently intractable [resistant] to other forms of treatment. Stem cells … may produce revolutionary changes in medicine seen only rarely in human history."

THE OTHER STEM CELLS

>> *U.S. News and World Report*
June 6, 2004

Like children, human embryonic stem cells are filled with potential but difficult to control. ... Removed from their tightly programmed life as an embryo, they can multiply indefinitely in the lab in primitive form or they can be coaxed to differentiate into virtually any cell in the body—a nest of beating heart cells, for example. But inject them into intact animals, and they are just as likely to be rejected by the immune system. ... What may be saving embryonic stem cells from the political quagmire [predicament] are their increasingly compelling distant cousins, adult stem cells, which are quickly making regenerative medicine a dramatic reality.

The other major kind of stem cells—adult stem cells—are like embryonic stem cells because they have not yet become specialized. But there are major differences between the two types of stem cells.

First, adult stem cells are not found in embryos. They exist in fully formed people and animals. Adult stem cells are also found in many different parts of the body. Scientists have found them in bone marrow, blood, the cornea and retina of the eyes, the liver, the skin, the digestive tract, and other places.

These adult stem cells help the body repair injuries. If you scrape your knee, an adult stem cell in the skin receives a signal. In response, the cell transforms into a skin cell and helps regenerate, or regrow, the damaged skin tissue.

Adult stem cells can be mixed with other cells to repopulate the bone marrow in a cancer patient.

LIMITATIONS OF ADULT STEM CELLS

The ability of adult stem cells to regenerate makes them seem as useful as embryonic stem cells. However, researchers have found that adult stem cells have certain disadvantages when compared to embryonic cells. First, adult stem cells have less plasticity—the ability of a stem cell to transform into other kinds of cells. An average adult stem cell cannot transform into a cell type that is different from its own. An adult stem cell in the skin transforms only into a skin cell. Similarly, an adult stem cell in the liver can only become a liver cell.

Also, the transformation process for adult stem cells is slightly more

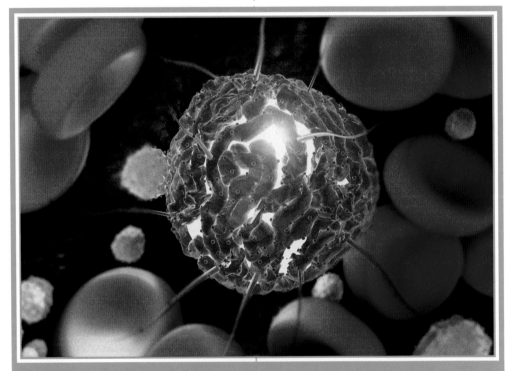

An embryonic stem cell has greater potential for research because it can become any type of cell, such as a red or white blood cell.

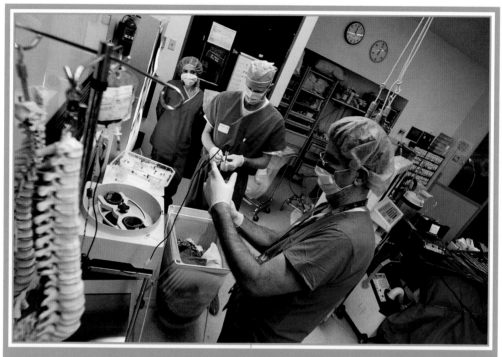

Dennis Kennedy, a nurse at the Banner Desert Children's Hospital in Mesa, Arizona, transferred bone marrow into a machine. The machine filtered out the stem cells, which were used to help grow new bone in cancer patients.

complicated than the one for embryonic stem cells. An embryonic stem cell turns directly into a specific kind of cell, but an adult stem cell first enters a stage where it is known as a precursor cell. Over time, the precursor cell matures into a skin cell, liver cell, or other kind of cell.

Another limitation of adult stem cells is that they are few in number compared to normal cells. Adult stem cells in bone marrow—known as hematopoietic cells, or blood stem cells—are a good example. Only one of these cells exists for every 10,000 bone marrow cells. So adult stem cells are harder to find and collect in usable numbers than embryonic stem cells. Another problem is that adult stem cells become harder to find as a person ages.

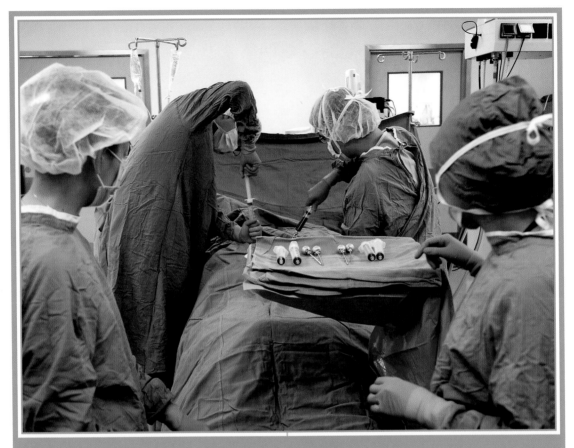

Bone marrow donations are performed in operating rooms in hospitals throughout the world. A large needle is used to extract the bone marrow, which can then be cryopreserved for later use.

Another disadvantage of using adult stem cells for medical purposes is that they are difficult to grow in a lab. These cells often take months to grow and mature. A sick patient who is waiting for these cells might die before the cells are ready.

A SIGNIFICANT ADVANTAGE

Despite these limitations, adult stem cells have one important advantage: They could be specially grown for individual patients. This would greatly reduce or even eliminate tissue rejection. "We could isolate the adult stem cells from a patient," the National Institutes of Health explains. Then the scientists could "coax them to divide and direct their specialization," or growth, into the kinds of cells that are desired. Finally, the cells could be transplanted back into the patient. Using this procedure, "it is unlikely that such cells would be rejected."

One exception would be patients with genetic disorders such as cystic fibrosis, Tay-Sachs disease, or muscular dystrophy. In such disorders, a defect is present in the patient's genes—sections of DNA that house the blueprints for life. Because genes exist in every cell in a person's body,

any defects in the genes also exist in all of that person's cells. So using the patient's own cells to grow new stem cells would only fuel the disease.

For most patients, adult stem cells may be beneficial. Many scientists are currently working with these cells. Harvey Lodish, a professor and medical researcher at the Massachusetts Institute of Technology, was able to get adult stem cells to multiply much faster than had previously been possible.

Lodish and other researchers caution that the full potential of adult stem cells remains uncertain. It is not yet clear whether these cells will ever show as much promise as embryonic stem cells for medical purposes.

Careful research into both embryonic and adult stem cells is ongoing. So far, the results show that these special cells hold a great deal of promise in fighting and curing a long list of dreaded diseases.

NOW YOU KNOW

Muscular dystrophy affects about 20,000 people in the United States, and an estimated 1 million people suffer from it worldwide.

STEM CELL ADVANCES OFFER HOPE TO BACK UP THE HYPE

>>> *National Geographic*
December 4, 2006

[We] have seen major breakthroughs in stem cell research, including the restoration of vision in blind mice and the use of human stem cells to produce insulin "naturally" in diabetic mice. Human stem cell treatments for these and other diseases may in some cases be at least a decade away. But each new discovery has added to the notion that stem cell research is showing increasing signs of living up to the hype surrounding it. ... Stem cells are primal cells that have the potential to transform into various cells and tissues found in the human body. They could potentially be used to repair tissue, grow new organs, or lead to treatments for a wide range of ailments.

The exciting field of stem cell research is relatively new, but it was built on centuries of learning about cells and how they work. Building on prior cell research, researchers at the Ontario Cancer Institute found evidence of stem cells in mice in 1963. Scientists were unable to isolate these cells until 1988. The breakthrough occurred at Stanford University where Irving Weissman separated adult stem cells from other cells in mice. Four years later, Weissman and his associates isolated adult stem cells in human blood.

Irving Weissman is the director of the Institute of Stem Cell Biology and Regenerative Medicine at Stanford University in California.

Meanwhile, in 1981, two research teams—one at the University of California in San Francisco and the other at the University of Cambridge in England—observed embryonic stem cells in mice. One member of the San Francisco team, Gail Martin, coined the term *embryonic stem cell*, or ES cell. In 1998, at the University of Wisconsin, James Thomson and his colleagues removed stem cells from an embryo and grew them in their lab. Since that time, many other important advances in stem cell research have occurred in labs around the world. Among the countries in the forefront of this research are the United Kingdom, Japan, Israel, Sweden, Belgium, China, and the United States.

THE HISTORY OF STEM CELLS

Cytology, the study of cells, began in 1665. In that year, English scientist Robert Hooke used a primitive microscope to make the first observation of cells. Hooke also coined the term *cell*. Over the centuries that followed, the knowledge about cells expanded. Researchers identified the parts of cells and discovered that the human body contains more than 220 different kinds of cells. However, they did not understand how this wide variety of cells developed. It was not until the early 1900s that scientists began to suspect the existence of stem cells. At first they called them "seed cells." The theory was that special cells acted like seeds for the formation of other cells.

Hooke sketched his observations of the structure of plant cells.

FIGHTING CANCER AND PARALYSIS

Although most of these advances took place in recent years, they have already produced significant medical breakthroughs. One is the use of stem cells to fight leukemia and other cancers, especially in children. Leukemia is cancer of the blood or bone marrow. Immature or abnormal blood cells build up in the body of a person with leukemia.

To fight the disease, doctors can harvest stem cells from human blood.

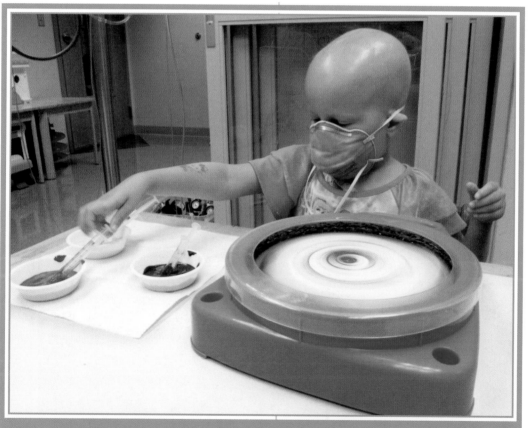

A leukemia patient's immune system is weakened because of extensive treatment to remove the cancerous cells. Therefore, the patient must wear a protective mask in public places to avoid getting sick. The treatment also causes the patient's hair to fall out.

HEADLINE SCIENCE

These cells are made in the bone marrow, the spongy material inside bones. This process is called a blood stem cell transplant, or SCT. The stem cells can come either from a relative or a stranger. But the chances of success are higher when the donor is a sibling, especially a twin brother or sister.

In an SCT, the stem cells are harvested through a procedure called apheresis. The donor is connected to a machine that separates some of the stem cells from the rest of the person's blood. According to a leading support group for leukemia patients, on the day of the harvest, the donor goes to the apheresis room and has an IV placed in both arms. "Most collection centers try to make the donor as comfortable as possible" by providing chairs, music, TV, "or other items of comfort."

During an apheresis study at Yale Medical School in Connecticut, blood was exposed to ultraviolet light to kill certain microbes.

During the session, some of the donor's blood moves through an IV and into the machine. There the blood spins around fast enough to separate out the stem cells. These are collected in a small bag, after which the blood flows back into the donor's body through a second IV. There is little or no pain throughout the process.

The harvested stem cells precede various kinds of normal blood cells, and they have the ability to transform into healthy blood cells. The doctors inject the harvested stem cells into a leukemia patient after most of the original bone marrow cells are destroyed from chemotherapy or radiation. In many cases, these injected stem cells grow into healthy new cells.

Strides have also been made toward using stem cells to repair spinal cord injuries and cure

Cody Unser, who was paralyzed from the waist down, spoke at a news conference in Washington, D.C., to promote stem cell research.

paralysis. Long nerve cells called neurons run down the spinal cord. Neurons carry messages from the brain to the limbs and other body parts. If the spinal cord is damaged, the messages cannot get through, causing the person to become paralyzed.

In 2000, a Johns Hopkins University medical team led by Douglas Kerr experimented with paralyzed mice and rats. The researchers grew a batch of neural stem cells. They then injected these cells into the fluid in the rodents' spines. "After 8 weeks, we saw a definite functional improvement in half of the mice and rats," Kerr reported. "From 5 to 7 percent of the stem cells that migrated to the spinal cord appeared to differentiate into nerve cells. … Now we're working to explain how such an apparently small number of nerve cells can make such a relatively large improvement in function."

Because mice have a genetic makeup similar to humans, they are used by stem cell biologists in experiments.

This experiment has since been repeated by other researchers. Scientists and doctors believe that similar techniques will one day cure human spinal cord injuries. This was the hope voiced by actor Christopher Reeve, who played Superman in several Hollywood films. Reeve was paralyzed after falling from a horse in 1995. Until his death in 2004, he frequently urged politicians and others to fund stem cell research.

James Thomson (from left), John Gearhart of the Institute for Cell Engineering at Johns Hopkins University, and Christopher Reeve delivered a strong message of support for stem cell research at the National Press Club in Washington, D.C., the year before Reeve's death.

FUTURE STEM CELL CURES

Reeve pointed out that paralysis like his is only one of many medical conditions that stem cells might someday cure. "These tiny cells," he said, "hold the promise to treat and potentially cure diseases and disorders that have troubled all of our lives." Among the many devastating conditions Reeve listed are heart disease, diabetes, Parkinson's disease, Alzheimer's disease, and various genetic diseases.

The first of these, heart disease, is often caused by damage to or loss of heart tissue during a heart attack. Researchers hope to eventually grow embryonic stem cells into healthy heart muscle cells. These cells would be injected into the patient's heart.

Within weeks or months, the new cells would repair the damage and restore normal heart function.

There is similar hope for diabetes patients. Diabetes is a condition where a person has high blood sugar. Diabetes is usually caused by the inability of the pancreas to produce enough insulin—a hormone that regulates the amount of sugar in the blood. Researchers hope to be able to grow embryonic stem cells into healthy pancreas cells. Injected into the pancreas, they will begin producing insulin.

Some medical experts believe Parkinson's disease might someday be eliminated in the same way. This illness occurs when nerve cells in the brain stop producing

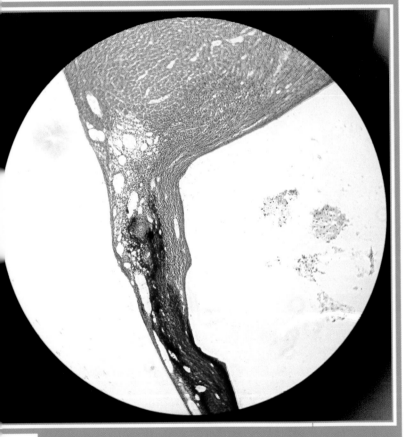

Human heart stem cells (blue) were used to repair rat heart cells (pink) at John Hopkins University.

HEADLINE
SCIENCE

Boxing legend Muhammad Ali (left) and actor Michael J. Fox urged a Senate subcommittee to continue funding Parkinson's disease research.

dopamine—a chemical that helps the body control the muscles. A person who does not have enough dopamine experiences tremors (shaking) and/or slowed speech.

Eventually it may be possible to grow embryonic stem cells into dopamine-producing nerve cells. When injected into a person suffering from Parkinson's disease, they might make enough dopamine to reduce or eliminate the symptoms. Michael J. Fox, star of the *Back to the Future* films, is one of almost 1 million Americans with Parkinson's disease. He believes that stem cell therapy will someday be a standard treatment for this and other diseases that are now incurable. ◤

UNTANGLING BIOTECH ISSUES: CLONING IS RESEARCH FIELD ENTIRELY SEPARATE FROM STEM CELLS

>>> *San Francisco Chronicle*
December 3, 2001

Controversial efforts to clone human embryos have run headlong into the stem-cell debate, thoroughly confusing anybody who has yet to figure out just what cloning has to do with stem cells anyway. Even some of the pioneers in the field [are] scratching their heads. ... [A]lthough cloning and stem cells can be intertwined, they are distinctly separate fields of research. Not all stem cells come from embryos. And not all cloning is designed to create genetically carbon-copied organisms, human or otherwise. Experts say such distinctions are becoming more important than ever as cutting-edge biology triggers a new cycle of ethical and political debate.

In recent years, many people have mistakenly considered stem cell research to be the same as the controversial technique of cloning. The confusion comes from three different areas. First, both stem cell research and cloning involve the use of embryonic stem cells. Second, both fields use a lab technique called somatic cell nuclear transfer (SCNT). Finally, some researchers coined the term *therapeutic cloning* to describe their work with embryonic stem cells. Perhaps more than anything else, this created the impression that stem cell research is about cloning.

While it is true that both stem cell research and cloning use embryonic

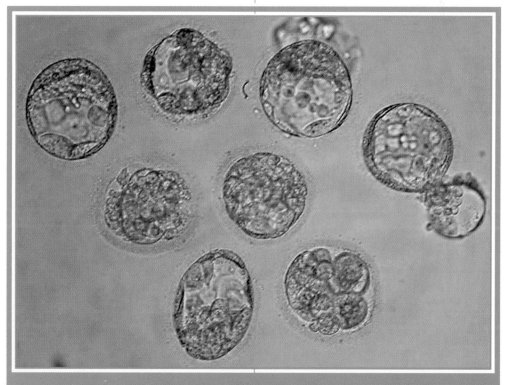

In 2004, Woo Suk Hwang and other researchers from Seoul, South Korea, claimed to have cloned human embryos to be used for stem cell research. However, in early 2006, a panel at Seoul National University disproved the claim.

stem cells and SCNT, they do so for different purposes. The goal of cloning is to use nuclear transfer to create a new person or animal. For that reason, it is often called "reproductive cloning." In contrast, researchers who pursue therapeutic cloning have no intention of making new humans or animals. Their goal is to use SCNT to create embryonic stem cells and tissues to cure various diseases and disorders.

Many scientists feel that this confusion between the two fields has made their work more difficult. This is because reproductive cloning is extremely controversial and banned in most countries. Hoping to clarify the differences between cloning and stem cell research, a number of scientists have stopped using the term therapeutic cloning. Instead, they call it "nuclear transfer" (NT).

As demonstrated by a billboard in St. Louis, Missouri, cloning continues to be a highly controversial subject throughout the world.

Starfish can completely regenerate from a single arm.

REPRODUCTIVE CLONING

A clear understanding of cloning is the first step in recognizing the difference between cloning and stem cell research. A clone is an exact copy of a plant, animal, or person. It comes from a single parent and has the same genes as that parent. Strawberries and ivy are examples of plants that naturally reproduce by cloning.

Starfish and planaria worms are animals that naturally reproduce by cloning.

In the late 20th century, some scientists began trying to clone higher animals—especially mammals—artificially. To do this, they developed the nuclear transfer process. It was SCNT that produced the first cloned mammal—Dolly the sheep—in 1996.

DOLLY THE SHEEP

The Roslin Institute researchers took an unfertilized egg from a female sheep and removed its genetic material. They also took an adult mammary gland cell, with its genetic material intact, from another sheep. When the two cells were combined, they grew into an embryo. The researchers implanted it into the uterus of a third sheep. A few months later, Dolly was born. She was a nearly exact replica of the sheep that had supplied the genetic material.

NOW YOU KNOW

In 2002, a Canadian corporation—Clonaid—claimed it had cloned a human baby girl. However, the corporation offered no proof, and most experts think the claim is untrue.

The event took place at the Roslin Institute in Roslin, Scotland. Since that time, SCNT has been used to clone many other kinds of animals, including cows, horses, pigs, and mice. To date, no human beings have been cloned.

THERAPEUTIC CLONING, OR NUCLEAR TRANSFER

Stem cell researchers also use SCNT. They, too, take an unfertilized egg and remove its genetic material. They also combine the egg with an adult cell to produce an embryo. However, they do not implant the embryo into a living animal or person.

Instead, the stem cell researchers use the newly formed embryo to create a new stem cell line. Their goal is to obtain as many healthy embryonic stem cells as they can. These cells are intended for use in two main areas. One is to study crippling diseases—especially genetic disorders—and the other is to develop cures for such diseases.

For example, cystic fibrosis is caused by defective genes in a person's cells. Researchers have isolated these genes, but they do not yet understand why they become defective. To study

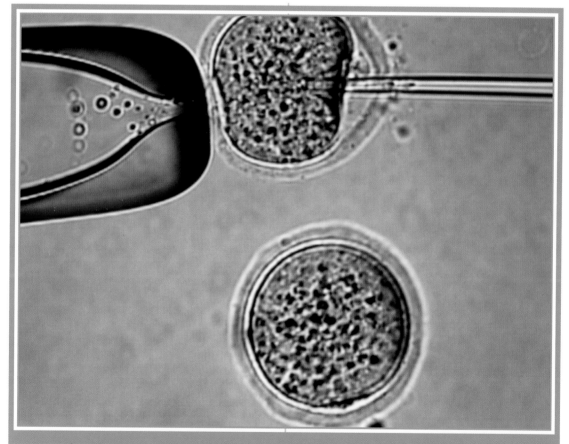

The genetic material in a mouse egg (upper center) was removed by a pipette (upper left) during nuclear transfer. A needle (right) was then used to insert an adult cell into the mouse cell.

them, scientists can take a cell from a cystic fibrosis patient. They then use SCNT to create a line of embryonic stem cells, all having the same defective genes. These cells can be used in lab experiments to find treatments and cures for the disease. One cure might involve creating new lines of healthy cells that could be injected into the patient, replacing his or her defective cells.

One major advantage of this approach to curing disease is that it would eliminate the problem of a person's immune system rejecting the foreign tissue. According to the International Society for Stem Cell Research:

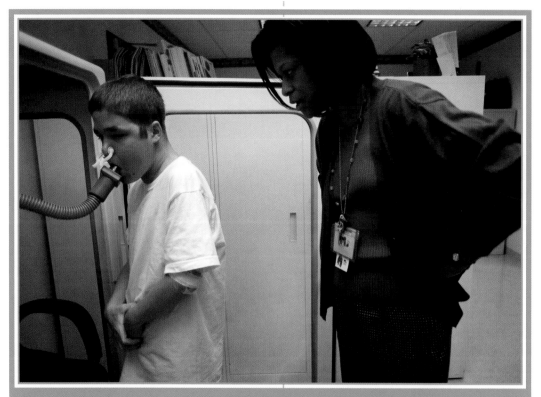

A boy with cystic fibrosis took a lung capacity test, which determines how much air his lungs can hold. Cystic fibrosis is the most common deadly genetic disease in the United States.

In 2007, California Governor Arnold Schwarzenegger (left) shook hands with the recipients of $45 million in grants from the California Institute for Regenerative Medicine.

Therapeutic cloning would allow the production of cells and tissues matching each individual patient because the donated nucleus would come from the patient. Thus, the cells would genetically match the patient and would not elicit rejection when they are transplanted into the patient.

For these reasons, stem cell researchers are extremely hopeful about the future. They believe their work will lead to cures for terrible illnesses that presently cause the suffering and/or deaths of millions of people.

"EMBRYO ETHICS"

Boston Globe
April 8, 2007

As the Senate prepares to take up stem cell legislation this week, Congress and the president are at odds over a tangled question at the boundary of science, ethics, and religion. President Bush has restricted federal funding of embryonic stem cell research, and last year [2006] cast the first veto of his presidency when Congress tried to ease the restriction. ... The main arguments are by now familiar. Proponents argue that embryonic stem cell research holds great promise for understanding and curing diabetes, Parkinson's disease, spinal cord injury, and other debilitating conditions. Opponents argue that the research is unethical, because deriving the stem cells destroys the blastocyst, an unimplanted human embryo at the sixth to eighth day of development.

Polls have shown that many Americans agree with President George W. Bush's stance on stem cell research. He believes that stem cells have potential to cure diseases, but he believes that most of the research should use adult stem cells because they do not involve human embryos. In his view, using embryonic stem cells destroys the embryos, which he sees as potential human beings. Therefore, he views most embryonic stem cell research as unethical. Bush's restriction of federal funding for such research and his veto of Congress's attempt to lift that restriction were based on these beliefs.

In 2006, President George W. Bush announced his decision to veto a bill that would increase federal funding for embryonic stem cell research. Families who had adopted frozen embryos attended the news conference with their children.

U.S. House Speaker Nancy Pelosi (seated) signed the Stem Cell Research Enhancement Act on June 7, 2007. Bush vetoed the bill 13 days later.

Bush had allowed one exception after being pressured by the scientific and medical communities. In 2001, he approved federal funding for 64 embryonic stem cell lines that already existed. Using these cell lines would not create or destroy any new embryos, he pointed out. Some scientists complained that some of those lines were too old and less practical than fresher ones. Also, since that time many of the original 64 lines have become unusable. The U.S. National Institutes of Health reports that only about 22 of the lines are still viable. Therefore, those scientists argue that new lines of embryonic stem cells are badly needed to reach the technology's great potential.

FOR OR AGAINST

Bush's policy shows that the line between the two ethical sides of embryonic stem cell research has been sharply drawn. Whether for or against stem cell research, many people feel strongly that their position is ethically correct. Those in favor of the research, including many bioethicists, say that the needs of sick people should come first. In their view, embryos are not fully formed humans. Bioethicist Arthur Caplan puts it this way:

> *I'm not going to look at a person in a wheelchair and say, "Sorry, you have to stay in that wheelchair for the rest of your life because of my belief that the frozen embryos in my liquid nitrogen might have become life."*

The mother of a 9-year-old girl with juvenile diabetes showed her support for stem cell research outside the Capitol in Washington, D.C.

Protesters against stem cell research demonstrated outside a regenerative medicine and biotech industries building in San Diego, California.

On the other hand, opponents of embryonic stem cell research argue that embryos should be given the same rights as people. They believe these rights should be protected by society and the government. In addition, they argue that embryonic stem cell research has been overhyped. Some people are not convinced that the research will deliver on its promises. One critic said:

Individuals suffering from chronic diseases have been misled into believing that a cure is around the corner in an effort to secure research funding. The voice of the suffering has been exploited to compel the public into supporting investigations that are speculative and unproven and that represent a significant departure from ethical standards that respect the sanctity of human life.

CAN RECENT ADVANCES END THE DEBATE?

These ethical concerns have prompted a number of scientists to try new approaches to using stem cells. In late 2007, British scientists announced that they had created embryos that were part human and part animal for medical research. They claimed they could extract viable stem cells from these embryos. Because the embryos are part animal, they stated that the usual ethical arguments do not apply. However, opponents of embryonic stem cell research immediately criticized these human-animal hybrids. They feared that weird monsters might be created in the lab. One observer noted:

HEADLINE SCIENCE

In early 2008, people from the Christian Concern for Our Nation marched outside the House of Lords in Westminster, England, to protest the use of human-animal embryos.

NOW YOU KNOW

Opinions about when an embryo can be defined as a human being vary greatly. The viewpoints range from when a fertilized egg begins dividing, to 14 days after conception, to birth.

Many expressed concern that the work constitutes meddling with nature ... and might lead to more troubling experiments. Others said they fear that some hybrid embryos—which scientists call chimeras, after the mythical Greek creature with a lion's head, a goat's body and a serpent's tail—might be transferred to women's wombs, where they might develop.

In 2005, an American biotech company said it had found a way to remove stem cells from an embryo without destroying the embryo. But critics argue that this makes no difference. They argue that removing cells might damage the embryo.

ACHIEVING A BALANCE?

The debate over stem cell research is far from over. Meanwhile, research continues in labs around the world. Several are government funded. Some countries that have strong ethical concerns impose restrictions on these labs. Among the more restrictive countries are the United States, Ireland, Poland, Germany, and Italy. The nations that have fewer ethical concerns, rules, and restrictions include the United Kingdom, Australia, China, India, Sweden, Belgium, and Japan.

Whatever their nationality, the scientists involved in stem cell research realize they cannot ignore the ethical judgments of other people. Many of them have stated their hope of achieving some sort of balance between medical progress and the ethical worries about their research. In the words of Australia's government-funded biotechnology team:

Chapter 5: *The Ethics Debate*

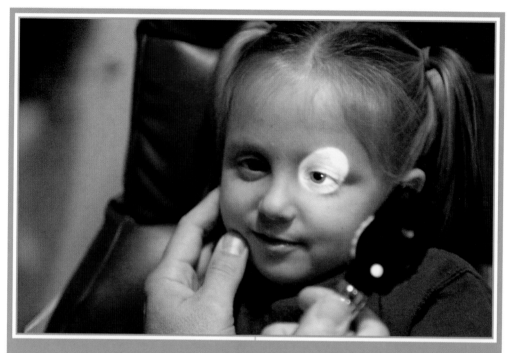

The sight of a young girl who was blind since birth began to show improvement after receiving stem cell treatments in China in 2007.

This issue is highly emotive [emotional] and it will always be necessary to consider all opinions and to balance the harm that might be done against the potential good this research may provide for those suffering from debilitating diseases. ... All scientists are aware that they must undertake their work ethically and within the bounds of the law, and these can vary from country to country.

More and more people are thinking about the potential of stem cells. Some worry that using this new technology may sometimes be unethical. But others feel that its advantages will far outweigh its disadvantages. Almost certainly, the next 10 to 20 years will show whether stem cells can fulfill the great promise they seem to hold.

1963
Scientists find the first conclusive evidence of stem cells in mice

1981
Embryonic stem cells are first observed and isolated in mice

1987
The Catholic Church states that some stem cell research presents problems because human embryos are human beings and must be respected as such

1995
Researchers isolate embryonic stem cells in monkeys

1996
The Roslin Institute in Scotland creates Dolly the sheep, the first mammal cloned from adult cells from a living creature

1998
A team at the University of Wisconsin is first to isolate human embryonic stem cells

2000
A team at Johns Hopkins University successfully uses stem cells to produce movement in paralyzed rats and mice

2001
U.S. President George W. Bush allows research to go forward on a few existing embryonic stem cell lines

2002
Bush allows researchers at federally funded labs to continue with stem cell research as long as the work is privately funded

2004
Arnold Schwarzenegger, governor of California, backs an initiative to spend $3 billion on stem cell research

2005
An American biotech company finds a way to extract stem cells from an embryo without destroying the embryo

2006
Bush vetoes a congressional bill that would have lifted some of his restrictions on stem cell research

2007
British researchers announce that they have created embryos that are half human and half animal for medical stem cell research

2008
Researchers turn human embryonic stem cells into cells that make insulin, raising hopes for finding a cure for diabetes

Timeline

GLOSSARY

adult stem cells
stem cells that exist in many parts of the body and help damaged tissue regenerate

bioethicists
experts in medicine, philosophy, law, and other fields who advise doctors, politicians, companies, and others about the ethics of biology-related issues

biotech
having to do with technology designed for biological research

cell line
all of the stem cells grown from a single stem cell

clone
living organism that grows from the genes of a single parent and is genetically identical to that parent

differentiated cells
cells that have already transformed into specific cell types

embryonic stem cells
stem cells that come from embryos

embryos
groups of cells that exist at an early stage in the life of a human or animal

pancreas
organ of the body that produces insulin, a hormone that regulates blood sugar

paralysis
reduction or loss of movement, usually caused by damage to the spine or nervous system

Parkinson's disease
condition in which the body loses control of the muscles and the person experiences tremors (shaking) and/or slowed speech

plasticity
ability of a stem cell to transform into other kinds of cells

pluripotent
ability of a stem cell to become almost any kind of cell; characteristic of early embryonic stem cells

precursor cell
cell that forms from an adult stem cell and soon transforms into a specific cell type

somatic cell nuclear transfer (SCNT)
lab process in which the genetic material is removed from an egg, which is then fused with the genetic material from another cell; this produces a new cell that can divide and form an embryo

FURTHER RESOURCES

ON THE WEB

For more information on this topic, use FactHound.

1. Go to *www.facthound.com*
2. Type in this book ID: 0756533716
3. Click on the *Fetch It* button.

FactHound will find the best Web sites for you.

FURTHER READING

Allman, Toney. *Stem Cells*. Yankton, S.D.: Erickson Press, 2007.

Black, Laura. *The Stem Cell Debate: The Ethics and Science Behind the Research*. Berkeley Heights, N.J.: Enslow Publishers, 2006.

Morgan, Sally. *From Microscopes to Stem Cell Research: Discovering Regenerative Medicine*. Chicago: Heinemann Library, 2006.

Tesar, Jenny. *Stem Cells*. San Diego: Blackbirch Press, 2003.

LOOK FOR OTHER BOOKS IN THIS SERIES:

Climate Crisis: The Science of Global Warming

Goodbye, Gasoline: The Science of Fuel Cells

Great Shakes: The Science of Earthquakes

Nature Interrupted: The Science of Environmental Chain Reactions

Rise of the Thinking Machines: The Science of Robots

SOURCE NOTES

Chapter 1: "Reeve's Legacy: Stem Cell Research." MSNBC. 11 Oct. 2004. 9 May 2008. www.msnbc.msn.com/id/6224513/

Chapter 2: Bernadine Healy. "The Other Stem Cells." *U.S. News and World Report*. 6 June 2004. 20 Oct. 2007. http://health.usnews.com/usnews/health/articles/040614/14healy.htm

Chapter 3: Stefan Lovgren. "Stem Cell Advances Offer Hope to Back Up the Hype." *National Geographic*. 4 Dec. 2006. 2 Nov. 2007. http://news.nationalgeographic.com/news/2006/12/061206-stem-cells.html

Chapter 4: Carl T. Hall. "Untangling Biotech Issues: Cloning is Research Field Entirely Separate from Stem Cells." *San Francisco Chronicle*. 3 Dec. 2001. 22 Sept. 2007. http://sfgate.com/cgi-bin/article.cgi?f=/c/a/2001/12/03/MN138336.DTL&type=science

Chapter 5: Michael J. Sandel. "Embryo Ethics." *Boston Globe*. 8 April 2007. 25 Sept. 2007. www.boston.com/news/globe/ideas/articles/2007/04/08/embryo_ethics/

ABOUT THE AUTHOR

Don Nardo has published several books on modern scientific discoveries and phenomena. He has also written biographies of scientists Charles Darwin and Tycho Brahe. Nardo lives with his wife, Christine, in Massachusetts.

INDEX